LAYERS OF LEARNING

YEAR TWO • UNIT TEN

BURGUNDY, VENICE, & SPAIN
SWITZERLAND
NERVES
OIL PAINTS

Published by HooDoo Publishing
United States of America
© 2014 Layers of Learning
Copies of maps or activities may be made for a particular family or classroom.
ISBN 978-1495306365

UNITS AT A GLANCE: TOPICS FOR ALL FOUR YEARS OF THE LAYERS OF LEARNING PROGRAM

1	History	Geography	Science	The Arts
1	Mesopotamia	Maps & Globes	Planets	Cave Paintings
2	Egypt	Map Keys	Stars	Egyptian Art
3	Europe	Global Grids	Earth & Moon	Crafts
4	Ancient Greece	Wonders	Satellites	Greek Art
5	Babylon	Mapping People	Humans in Space	Poetry
6	The Levant	Physical Earth	Laws of Motion	List Poems
7	Phoenicians	Oceans	Motion	Moral Stories
8	Assyrians	Deserts	Fluids	Rhythm
9	Persians	Arctic	Waves	Melody
10	Ancient China	Forests	Machines	Chinese Art
11	Early Japan	Mountains	States of Matter	Line & Shape
12	Arabia	Rivers & Lakes	Atoms	Color & Value
13	Ancient India	Grasslands	Elements	Texture & Form
14	Ancient Africa	Africa	Bonding	African Tales
15	First North Americans	North America	Salts	Creative Kids
16	Ancient South America	South America	Plants	South American Art
17	Celts	Europe	Flowering Plants	Jewelry
18	Roman Republic	Asia	Trees	Roman Art
19	Christianity	Australia & Oceania	Simple Plants	Instruments
20	Roman Empire	You Explore	Fungi	Composing Music

2	History	Geography	Science	The Arts
1	Byzantines	Turkey	Climate & Seasons	Byzantine Art
2	Barbarians	Ireland	Forecasting	Illumination
3	Islam	Arabian Peninsula	Clouds & Precipitation	Creative Kids
4	Vikings	Norway	Special Effects	Viking Art
5	Anglo Saxons	Britain	Wild Weather	King Arthur Tales
6	Charlemagne	France	Cells and DNA	Carolingian Art
7	Normans	Nigeria	Skeletons	Canterbury Tales
8	Feudal System	Germany	Muscles, Skin, & Cardiopulmonary	Gothic Art
9	Crusades	Balkans	Digestive & Senses	Religious Art
10	Burgundy, Venice, Spain	Switzerland	Nerves	Oil Paints
11	Wars of the Roses	Russia	Health	Minstrels & Plays
12	Eastern Europe	Hungary	Metals	Printmaking
13	African Kingdoms	Mali	Carbon Chem	Textiles
14	Asian Kingdoms	Southeast Asia	Non-metals	Vivid Language
15	Mongols	Caucasus	Gases	Fun With Poetry
16	Medieval China & Japan	China	Electricity	Asian Arts
17	Pacific Peoples	Micronesia	Circuits	Arts of the Islands
18	American Peoples	Canada	Technology	Indian Legends
19	The Renaissance	Italy	Magnetism	Renaissance Art I
20	Explorers	Caribbean Sea	Motors	Renaissance Art II

3	History	Geography	Science	The Arts
1	Age of Exploration	Argentina and Chile	Classification & Insects	Fairy Tales
2	The Ottoman Empire	Egypt and Libya	Reptiles & Amphibians	Poetry
3	Mogul Empire	Pakistan & Afghanistan	Fish	Mogul Arts
4	Reformation	Angola & Zambia	Birds	Reformation Art
5	Renaissance England	Tanzania & Kenya	Mammals & Primates	Shakespeare
6	Thirty Years' War	Spain	Sound	Baroque Music
7	The Dutch	Netherlands	Light & Optics	Baroque Art I
8	France	Indonesia	Bending Light	Baroque Art II
9	The Enlightenment	Korean Pen.	Color	Art Journaling
10	Russia & Prussia	Central Asia	History of Science	Watercolors
11	Conquistadors	Baltic States	Igneous Rocks	Creative Kids
12	Settlers	Peru & Bolivia	Sedimentary Rocks	Native American Art
13	13 Colonies	Central America	Metamorphic Rocks	Settler Sayings
14	Slave Trade	Brazil	Gems & Minerals	Colonial Art
15	The South Pacific	Australasia	Fossils	Principles of Art
16	The British in India	India	Chemical Reactions	Classical Music
17	Boston Tea Party	Japan	Reversible Reactions	Folk Music
18	Founding Fathers	Iran	Compounds & Solutions	Rococo
19	Declaring Independence	Samoa and Tonga	Oxidation & Reduction	Creative Crafts I
20	The American Revolution	South Africa	Acids & Bases	Creative Crafts II

4	History	Geography	Science	The Arts
1	American Government	USA	Heat & Temperature	Patriotic Music
2	Expanding Nation	Pacific States	Motors & Engines	Tall Tales
3	Industrial Revolution	U.S. Landscapes	Energy	Romantic Art I
4	Revolutions	Mountain West States	Energy Sources	Romantic Art II
5	Africa	U.S. Political Maps	Energy Conversion	Impressionism I
6	The West	Southwest States	Earth Structure	Impressionism II
7	Civil War	National Parks	Plate Tectonics	Post-Impressionism
8	World War I	Plains States	Earthquakes	Expressionism
9	Totalitarianism	U.S. Economics	Volcanoes	Abstract Art
10	Great Depression	Heartland States	Mountain Building	Kinds of Art
11	World War II	Symbols and Landmarks	Chemistry of Air & Water	War Art
12	Modern East Asia	The South States	Food Chemistry	Modern Art
13	India's Independence	People of America	Industry	Pop Art
14	Israel	Appalachian States	Chemistry of Farming	Modern Music
15	Cold War	U.S. Territories	Chemistry of Medicine	Free Verse
16	Vietnam War	Atlantic States	Food Chains	Photography
17	Latin America	New England States	Animal Groups	Latin American Art
18	Civil Rights	Home State Study	Instincts	Theater & Film
19	Technology	Home State Study II	Habitats	Architecture
20	Terrorism	America in Review	Conservation	Creative Kids

Unit 2-10

Printable Pack

This unit includes printables at the end. To make life easier for you we also created digital printable packs for each unit. To retrieve your printable pack for Unit 2-10, please visit

www.layers-of-learning.com/digital-printable-packs/

Put the printable pack in your shopping cart and use this coupon code:

4444UNIT2-10

Your printable pack will be free.

LAYERS OF LEARNING INTRODUCTION

This is part of a series of units in the Layers of Learning homeschool curriculum, including the subjects of history, geography, science, and the arts. Children from 1st through 12th can participate in the same curriculum at the same time – family school style.

The units are intended to be used in order as the basis of a complete curriculum (once you add in a systematic math, reading, and writing program). You begin with Year 1 Unit 1 no matter what ages your children are. Spend about 2 weeks on each unit. You pick and choose the activities within the unit that appeal to you and read the books from the book list that are available to you or find others on the same topic from your library. We highly recommend that you use the timeline in every history section as the backbone. Then flesh out your learning with reading and activities that highlight the topics you think are the most important.

Alternatively, you can use the units as activity ideas to supplement another curriculum in any order you wish. You can still use them with all ages of children at the same time.

When you've finished with Year One, move on to Year Two, Year Three, and Year Four. Then begin again with Year One and work your way through the years again. Now your children will be older, reading more involved books, and writing more in depth. When you have completed the sequence for the second time, you start again on it for the third and final time. If your student began with Layers of Learning in 1st grade and stayed with it all the way through she would go through the four year rotation three times, firmly cementing the information in her mind in ever increasing depth. At each level you should expect increasing amounts of outside reading and writing. High schoolers in particular should be reading extensively, and if possible, participating in discussion groups.

☺ ☻ ☻ These icons will guide you in spotting activities and books that are appropriate for the age of child you are working with. But if you think an activity is too juvenile or too difficult for your kids, adjust accordingly. The icons are not there as rules, just guides.

☺ GRADES 1-4
☻ GRADES 5-8
☻ GRADES 9-12

Within each unit we share:
- EXPLORATIONS, activities relating to the topic;
- EXPERIMENTS, usually associated with science topics;
- EXPEDITIONS, field trips;
- EXPLANATIONS, teacher helps or educational philosophies.

In the sidebars we also include Additional Layers, Famous Folks, Fabulous Facts, On the Web, and other extra related topics that can take you off on tangents, exploring the world and your interests with a bit more freedom. The curriculum will always be there to pull you back on track when you're ready.

You can learn more about how to use this curriculum at www.layers-of-learning.com/layers-of-learning-program/

UNIT TEN

BURGUNDY, VENICE, & SPAIN – SWITZERLAND – NERVES– OIL PAINTS

It suddenly struck me that that tiny pea, pretty and blue was the Earth. I put up my thumb and shut one eye, and my thumb blotted out the planet Earth. I didn't feel like a giant. I felt very, very small.
-Neil Armstrong

	LIBRARY LIST:
HISTORY	Search for: Duchy of Burgundy, Venice, Reconquista, Spanish Inquisition ☺ This is Venice by M. Sasek. Takes you on a tour of the modern city, but most of the landmarks are from medieval times. ☺ Bravo, Zan Angelo by Niki Daly. A troop of performers in Renaissance Italy. ☺ Gabriella's Song by Giselle Potter. Picture book of a Venetian girl making music. ☺ Vendela in Venice by Christina Bjork. A modern Swedish girl visits the city with her father and learns about the history and culture of the city. ☺ ☻ Prisoner of the Inquisition by Theresa Breslin. Historical fiction. ☺ ☻ A Tale of the Cid: and Other Stories of Knights and Chivalry by Andrew Lang. ☻ Thomas de Torquemada: Architect of Torture During the Spanish Inquisition by Eind A. Goldberg and Norman Itzkowitz. ☻ The Broken Bracelet by Gershon Kranzler. ☻ The Red Keep by Allen French. Adventure and intrigue in 12th century Burgundy. ☺ ☻ El Cid by Geraldine McCaughrean. Heroic Spanish knight of the Reconquista. ☻ Venice: A New History by Thomas F. Madden. ☻ Torquemada and the Spanish Inquisition by Rafael Sabatini.
GEOGRAPHY	Search for: Switzerland ☺ A Bell for Ursli: A Story from the Engradine in Switzerland. This is an old, traditional tale that Swiss kids have grown up with. It's the story of Ursli, who wants to find the biggest bell so he can lead the spring procession through his village. ☺ ☻ The Apple and the Arrow by Conrad Buff. ☺ ☻ Heidi by Johanna Spyri. ☺ Rollo in Switzerland by Jacob Abbott. Free on Kindle. ☻ Swiss Holiday by Elizabeth Yates. ☺ ☻ Banner in the Sky by James Ramsey Ullman. Mountaineering Adventure. ☺ ☻ The Spell of Switzerland by Nathan Haskell Dole. ☺ Switzerland by Frank Fox. Overview history of the people and the geography.

SCIENCE

Search for: brain, nervous system
- ☺ ☻ ● <u>Brain Anatomy Model</u> from Learning Resources. Plastic 3-d brain model.
- ☺ <u>How Does Your Brain Work?</u> by Don L. Curry. Very simple for little kids.
- ☺ <u>The Nervous System</u> by Christine Taylor Butler.
- ☺ <u>Use Your Brain</u> by Paul Showers.
- ☺ <u>Your Fantastic, Elastic Brain: Stretch It, Shape It</u> by JoAnne Deak PhD. Discusses brain anatomy and functions on a little kid level, but also how we learn and how making mistakes is essential to the process.
- ☺ ● <u>Dr. Frankenstein's Human Body Book</u> by Richard Walker. All body systems.
- ☺ ● <u>How To Be A Genius</u> from DK. Brain functions and how to train your brain.
- ☺ ● <u>The Brain: Our Nervous System</u> by Seymour Simon.
- ● <u>The Great Brain Book</u> by H.P. Newquist. Science mixed with anecdote, engaging.
- ☺ <u>The Human Brain Book</u> by Rita Carter. Pretty advanced stuff, but written for non-experts, from DK, lots of visuals.

THE ARTS

Search for: oil painting, Jan van Eyck
- ☺ ☻ ● <u>Art Masterpieces to Color: 60 Great Paintings from Botticelli to Picasso</u> by Marty Noble.
- ☺ ☻ ● <u>The Usborne Book of Famous Paintings</u> by Rosie Dickens.
- ☺ ● <u>13 Art Inventions Children Should Know</u> by Florian Heine.
- ☺ <u>The Usborne First Book of Art</u> by Rosie Dickens.
- ● <u>Art Treasury</u> by Rosie Dickens.
- ☺ <u>The Usborne Introduction to Art</u> by Rosie Dickens.
- ● <u>Name That Style: All About Isms in Art</u> by Bob Raczka.
- ☺ <u>The Annotated Mona Lisa</u> by Carol Strickland.
- ● <u>Jan Van Eyck: Renaissance Realist</u> by Till-Holger Borchert.
- ☺ <u>Oil Painting For Dummies</u> by Anita Marie Giddings and Sherry Stone Clifton. For kids who are serious about art.

HISTORY: BURGUNDY, VENICE, & SPAIN

BURGUNDY

The balance of power in Europe was always a tricky thing. The king needed nobles to administer his kingdom and protect it from foreign invaders, but the nobles were also the biggest threat to the king.

In 1361, the powerful Duke of Burgundy in France died without a male heir. The king of France, John the Good, inherited Burgundy through his mother's line and gave the duchy to his son, Philippe. Philippe and his heirs consolidated and expanded the power of the duchy until it rivaled the power of France herself. Burgundy was now in a position to thumb its nose at the other kings of Europe. It was an environment rife with intrigue and plotting, and amidst it all, the Duke Jean of Burgundy was murdered in 1419 on the orders of the Crown Prince of France. Unfortunately, France was in the middle of the Hundred Years War with England and the house of Burgundy was as closely related to the Kings of England as they were the Kings of France . . . royal intermarriages really made for some interesting situations. Burgundy decided to side with England for the remainder of the war, a decision fatal to the fortunes of France. England and Burgundy dominated the war until a young girl named Joan showed up on the scene.

This is one of the Ducal Homes of the Burgundians.

Burgundy wasn't only militarily strong though, it was also the poshest of the posh places in Europe. The duchy was the center of arts and sciences. Learned and skilled men and brilliant women gathered in her halls to be scintillating and intelligent in front of each other. Jan Van Eyck, the great painter, was the court painter of Burgundy.

By 1476, when Duchess Marie of Burgundy married Prince Maximilian of Hapsburg, the Duchy of Burgundy was sprawling from the Netherlands down to central France and covered as much land in the Holy Roman Empire as it did in France herself. When Marie's father, Duke Charles the Bold, died in 1477, the Hapsburgs claimed the Burgundian lands, but so did the King of France. They fought about it for awhile, but eventually the lands became divided between France and the Holy Roman Empire.

VENICE

Venice was founded during Roman times by the tribe called the Veneti. The Veneti held their lands in the north of the Italian peninsula, right on the path of invaders such as Hannibal and the Barbarians. After they had been overrun yet again, they moved their city into a swamp, nice and out-of-the-way and inaccessible without boats. Since not many invaders crossing the Alps had boats, they were left at peace at last. The peace created an environment for prosperity.

The Piazzetta from the Bacino di San Marco by Caspar van Wittel (c. 1700)

Venice grew from a barely surviving village of fishermen to a world-wide trading center by 1100. Venetian ships sailed all over the Mediterranean, up into the Black Sea, and north to England and the Netherlands. During the Crusades, Venetian

Famous Folks

Margaret of Dampierre married Philippe The Bold in 1369. She was the only heir and countess of Flanders, Nevers, Rethel, Artoise, and Brabant. When her father died she and her husband inherited all these duchies and passed them on to their eldest son. Burgundy was growing and so was its power.

Teaching Tip

Hands-on learning and projects are great retention tools, but the best of intentions go down the drain if you don't do a little planning ahead to make it happen. Peruse through the unit and jot down any supplies and books you need ahead of time so you aren't stressed when you're in the middle of the unit and can't find your stuff.

ships were hired to carry the knights and all their train across the Mediterranean to Palestine. The Venetians were there when Byzantium (supposedly their allies . . . oops!) was sacked and looted. Venice brought home ships full of treasure from that little excursion. Even though Venice didn't own much land, they owned nearly all the business and all the trade. They were extremely powerful, extremely wealthy, and extremely independent.

SPAIN

Most of the Iberian Peninsula had been overrun by the Muslim invaders from North Africa, known as the Moors. Around 1031, Christian kingdoms in the far north of Spain began to push back against the Muslim invaders, and by 1235 the Moors held only Granada in the far south.

Granada surrendering to Isabella and Ferdinand
by Francisco Pradilla y Ortiz (1882)

Spain was divided during this time into several independent kingdoms including Aragon, Castile, and Navarre. In 1469, Isabella, princess and heir of Castile, married Ferdinand, Prince and heir of Aragon. When their fathers died in their respective kingdoms, Ferdinand and Isabella agreed to rule as co-rulers over the newly united kingdoms. Now that their power was consolidated at home, they wished to make the final push and drive the Moors back to North Africa. A step toward doing this was to make sure that all their citizens were Catholic.

They received permission from the pope to establish courts of inquisition and they proceeded to use their religious authority for political purposes, persecuting, forcing conversions, and driving people out of Spain. During this time the large Jewish population of Spain, who were among the most learned of Spain's peoples, left en mass and most of them settled in the cosmopolitan Muslim city of Constantinople, where they were a great addition to the city and the court. In 1492, Ferdinand and Isabella succeeded in the reconquest of Spain. The inquisition would last three hundred and fifty years and engulf two continents before its end.

Maniera di bruciare quelli che furono condannati dalla Inquisizione

Inquisition: People being burned alive from a 17th century engraving.

☺ ☻ ☻ EXPLORATION: Timeline

Printable timeline squares can be found at the end of this unit.

- 1204 Venice finances the Fourth Crusade and makes a killing
- 1248 Christians reconquer most of Spain
- 1303 Crossbow proficiency by all adult males in Venice compulsory
- 1363-1304 Duke Philippe the Good of Burgundy rules
- 1348 Black Death devastates Venice
- 1381 Venice defeats Genoa to control all Mediterranean trade
- 1410-1411 Burgundy wars with Armagnac
- 1419 Duke Jean the Fearless of Burgundy is murdered
- 1450 Venice has over 3,000 merchant ships, fitted out for war when necessary
- 1469 Isabella and Ferdinand of Spain marry
- 1474 Isabella and Ferdinand co-rule Castile

- 1477 Marie of Burgundy marries Maximilian of Austria
- 1477-1493 France and Austria fight over Burgundy
- 1478 Spanish Inquisition is established
- 1479 Aragon and Castile are united
- 1482 Venice has become the printing capital of the world
- 1492 Conquest of Granada completed
- 1493 Maximilian becomes Holy Roman Emperor. Burgundy divided.

☻ ☻ EXPLORATION: Europe 15th Century Map

Color the Europe 15th Century Map from the end of this unit. We'll guide you through the map step by step. An example of the colored map for you to refer to is shown following the map instructions. This map shows Europe after the fall of the Byzantine Empire in 1461, but also the struggle between England and France that really ended in 1453.

1. Color all the water in blue. You should have memorized by now the Mediterranean, Black Sea, North Sea, and Baltic Sea, as well as the Atlantic Ocean. Can you name any other seas or waterways not labeled on the map?
2. Color the lands of Burgundy in purple. This includes the Duchy of Burgundy and also Flanders. There were other lands within the Holy Roman Empire and France that belonged to the Dukes of Burgundy from time to time as well. These are not shown on the map.
3. Color the Republic of Venice in yellow. There are two little territories at the north of the Italian peninsula, but also several islands in the eastern Mediterranean, including Crete and Lesbos. Check the colored map for the other Venetian Islands. These were used as trading centers for Venetian shipping. Venetian territories expanded and contracted some during this time as well.
4. Color the Spanish Kingdoms, Castile & Leon, Navarre, and Aragon, with three shades of orange, dark, medium and light. The Spanish are in the middle of shoving the Muslim kingdoms off the peninsula. Granada will be gone in 1492 and Spain will be united in one kingdom. The islands of Tviza, Majorca, Minorca, Sardinia, and Sicily all belong to Aragon at this point.
5. Next, you'll need five shades of green or bluish green to color the Muslim Kingdoms of Fez, Tunis, Mameluk, Granada, and the Ottoman Empire. The various Muslim kingdoms are still warring against Europe, but they begin their decline from this point.
6. Next, color Genoa in bright pink. Genoa is in northern Italy and is the major rival to Venice. They also have

colonies all over the Mediterranean including Corsica, Cyprus, a little slice of the coast of Bosnia, and the Genoese colonies on the north of the Black Sea. These colonies trade across the Silk Road into the Far East.

7. Color the Swiss Cantons in a bright red. The Swiss rebelled and broke off of the Holy Roman Empire in 1291. Each Swiss canton is independent but they have a loose confederation for mutual defense and trade. They will remain free to the present day.

8. Color France in dark blue. France's borders are in ebb and flow as they are in the middle of the Hundred Years War with England. On this map the English hold about half of what is present day France. We learned more about the Hundred Years War in Unit 2-7.

9. Color the English lands in a lighter red. England is ruling Aquitaine, northern France, and half of Ireland. They've been trying to conquer Scotland as well, but they never do. They'll finally be united with Scotland in 1603 when the Scottish King James inherits the English throne and becomes monarch of both nations.

10. Color Ireland in light green. Ireland, which had been subdued (sort of) by the Norman English in the 12th century, was reemerging as a completely Irish culture. The power of the Normans faded as the Norman English intermarried and became Irish. The English held only the city of Dublin and surrounding countryside by 1500.

11. Color Scotland in light purple. Scotland was also fighting for her freedom during the 15th century. In 2-7 we learned about these wars as well.

12. Color the Holy Roman Empire in light brown. The Holy Roman Empire is the heart of Europe and the strongest state. Later they will be challenged by France, but just now France is very weak.

13. Color the lands of the Teutonic Knights in light gray and Rhodes, the stronghold of the Knights Hospitalers in dark gray. The Teutonic Knights also hold a couple of islands in the Baltic Sea.

14. Color Lithuania in purple. Lithuania is still pagan. They are defending their borders against the Teutonic knights who are engaged in a holy war with them.

15. Color Novgorod and Russia in shades of green. The Russian kingdoms had been completely overrun by the Mongols (the Golden Horde), but now the Mongols are weakening and the Russians have carved out the beginnings of an empire.

16. Color the Khanate of the Golden Horde in light orange.

17. Color Poland in dark brown. Poland is a powerful Eastern

Teaching Tip

The point of coloring historical maps instead of merely looking at them is that you become engaged in the process, you remember better if you do than if you merely look. Also, it keeps the kids occupied while the teacher expostulates on all the tidbits of knowledge to take home.

Fabulous Fact

We'll learn more about the Mongols in Unit 2-15. They held the largest empire ever in the history of the world, stretching across most of Asia and half of Europe.

They were so fearsome that even the Muslims and Christians united to fight against them.

Additional Layer

Lithuania had close ties to Poland, the two kingdoms' monarchs intermarrying for alliances, mostly against the Teutonic Knights. In the end this was how Lithuania became Christianized, by adopting Polish customs and through intermarriage. In Unit 2-12 we'll learn more about these eastern kingdoms.

Additional Layer

The university system of Europe was already centuries old by the time Burgundy was at its height. Schooling happened almost exclusively in monasteries and convents. Schools were run by church men who taught the Trivium (grammar, logic, and rhetoric) and the Quadrivium (geometry, arithmetic, music and astronomy) in preparation for Theology, the highest learning of all. This sort of "learning for the glory of God" is uniquely Christian and goes far in explaining why Europe left the rest of the world technologically behind from the Renaissance on.

Additional Layer

In many ways it was harder at this period to be a noble than a commoner. Nobles had to marry where the king or their lord needed an alliance. Noble younger sons often had to forgo marriage and normal life altogether to live in a celibate life in a monastery where they could produce no heirs to divide up the lands of their fathers or provide rivals to their brothers.

European Christian kingdom at this point. But they will soon begin to fade and the country of Poland will not reappear until after World War I.

18. Color Hungary, Bosnia, and Albania in shades of blue.
19. Color the Papal States in golden brown, or bronze. The Popes actually ran their own country at this point in history. Today the vestige of that is the Vatican City.
20. Color Naples in red. Naples was run by a branch of the Norman kings who were originally Vikings.
21. Color Portugal and Denmark in yellow. Denmark owns a bunch of the coast of Sweden, all of Norway, the islands north of Scotland, and Iceland at this point.
22. Finally, color Sweden blue.

☺ ☺ ☺ EXPLORATION: Christmas at Burgundy.

Burgundy was one of the most wealthy and opulent courts in Europe. The Christmas celebrations there must have been amazing.

Festivities would start on December 25th, the day commemorating the birth of Christ. There would be a feast and a yule log, saved from the year before. They would have had roast goose and roast swan, wild boar and roast deer if the hunt had gone well, mince pies, gingerbread, yeast breads, plum pudding, thick rich stews, cheese, cake, and hot spiced drinks.

Trees outside the castle would be decorated with apples hung from the boughs in remembrance of Adam and Eve, the first parents in the Christian tradition. Inside, greenery of the countryside would be strewn over the hearths and tables, and candles lit everywhere. A nativity play would be performed and carols sung, though not in the church. On Christmas day three masses would be attended, the first at midnight, then again in the morning, and again in the afternoon. Then the festivities and feasting would continue on for the next twelve days, until January 6th, the day the wise men visited the baby Jesus. During this time in a rich castle such as Burgundy there would be entertainers, musicians, bards, and theater players.

Make a Burgundian Christmas feast by preparing ham, roast fowl, breads, pastie pies and hot spiced cider. Have sweet fruit pastries for dessert. Check www.godecookery.com for authentic medieval recipes. Decorate for the feast with cut out paper stars and candles. If you have a fireplace, burn a fire for the yule log.

☻ ☻ EXPLORATION: Venice

Venice was a city state, run by the noble families of the city. Here is the structure of the government:

Noble Families

↓

Great Council
Made up of nobles of the city, they elect the senate and appoint people to minor positions by vote.

↓

Senate
Consisting of 200-300 individuals, they had voting privileges, but little real power.

↓

Council of Ten
Elected from among the senate, they do the actual ruling of the city.

↓

Doge
Comes from Dux, latin for Duke, he is the elected ruler of the city, a lifetime appointment. The people of the city have the opportunity to reject or approve him by vote, upon his election by the senate.

In 1485 the ambassador of France said of Venice, "It is the most splendid city I have ever seen and the one that governs itself most

---

Famous Folks

The official court sculptor for Burgundy was Claus Sluter, who created the tombs for some of the Dukes of Burgundy, a task which took him most of his life. View some of his sculptures online and read more about him.

Claus Sluter's most famous sculpture, Well of Moses in the city of Dijon.

Fabulous Fact

By the Renaissance Venice was sort of the Vegas of Europe. It was where you went to party.

Additional Layer

Venice is best known for its trade, but it was also well known for glass, beads, silks, brocades, jewelry, armor, and eyeglasses. In fact, it was in Venice that Galileo invented his telescope because of a clever eyeglass maker there, who had created a simple telescope for his kids to play with. Galileo saw it, understood the potential for searching the night skies and made a grown-up version.

wisely." What kind of government did the city of Venice have? Monarchy? Republic? Feudal? Draw and illustrate the structure of the Venetian government.

☺ ☻ EXPLORATION: Venetian Buildings

Venice was built on several low lying marshy islands. The buildings could not be placed directly on the soggy, sinking soil, so they drove wood pilings in, tightly packed through the silt and sand to the firm clay beneath. Then on top of these pilings they built their city of stone. Because the pilings were completely submerged they did not rot away and the same pilings that were driven in over 500 years ago are there now.

This is a palace in Venice. See how the building sits right on the water? The wooden pilings are driven deeply in to the soft mud and completely submerged. The stone building is then placed directly on the pilings. Photo by Didier Descouens and shared under CC license on Wikimedia.

Make your own Venetian building with a pan, clay, water, toothpicks and sugar cubes. Spread a layer of clay in the bottom of a pan, like a cake pan. Pour water over the top until it is at least an inch higher than the clay. Push toothpicks, tight spaced into the clay to create a base for building on. Then carefully build a sugar cube building. If the sugar cubes touch the water they will disintegrate, just as the city of Venice must stay above water.

One of the most famous buildings is St. Mark's Basilica, built in 1063. For pictures and information about the Basilica, visit http://www.sacred-destinations.com/italy/venice-san-marco . You may also want to search for pictures of the Doge's Palace, St. Mark's Square, Palazzo Corner, and the Grand Canal.

☻ ☻ **EXPLORATION: City of Merchants**

Venice was a city of merchants and whatever they did, whether in war or in peace, was done with the view of making money. They held territories across the Mediterranean, especially in the east, for the sole purpose of controlling the trade and keeping pirates at bay. Even their involvement in the Crusades was merely a monetary contract to them and though they were Christian, it is not likely they were very motivated by pious feelings. Color a map showing the Venetian territories and routes in the Mediterranean. Use the Venice Territories and Trade map from the end of this unit.

☻ ☻ **EXPLORATION: Venetian Gondola**

Look up the history of gondolas in Venice, and as you read about them together, color the gondola coloring sheet from the printables at the end of the unit.

☻ ☻ ☻ **EXPLORATION: Gorgeous Glass**

Venice is famous for its glass. When the city of Constantinople was sacked several times over the years, many of its craftsmen fled to Venice, including many glass makers. Venetians perfected the art of glass making, and eventually it became such an important industry that the glass makers were as highly revered as the aristocracy. They were also not allowed to leave, lest the secrets of glass making get out and Venice lose its monopoly.

Find some examples of Venetian glassware online. Search for *Museo del Vertro*. This is the site of the Museum of Glass in

---

Additional Layer

Though embattled and overrun a few times, especially by Napoleon, Venice remained independent until 1866, when it joined the Italian states.

By that time Venice had been reduced by plague, battle and blockades to a shell of its former glory. The population was drastically reduced and the people left were destitute. They needed the Italian federation for physical protection and stability.

Fabulous Fact

Today on any given day in Venice there are more visitors than residents.

Additional Layer

Venice celebrated a "Marriage of the Sea" ceremony each year on Ascension Day. The Pope gave the Doge a consecrated ring and the Doge, with much ceremony, would lead a procession of boats out to the sea where the ring was cast in, "marrying" Venice to the Sea.

Painting by Canaletto (1730)

Additional Layer

Venice got not only the bones of St. Mark, but his horses too when they sacked Constantinople in 1204. This is how it happened. The Crusaders had commissioned ships from the Venetians but then were short of cash. So the Doge, said, "Hey, man, it's alright. We'll take you for free if you'll just capture a couple of cities for us." One of those cities turned out to be Constantinople, which the Venetians didn't want to rule—they just wanted the stuff. They made way more off the transport of the crusaders than they ever could have hoped, including the famous horses of St. Mark which they stuck on their church.

And Constantinople never recovered, falling to the Turks a century or so later.

Venice. The page is in Italian, but it is the images of glass you are interested in anyway. After you have looked at some actual Venetian glass, make this glass craft.

Purchase an inexpensive clear glass plate, cup, or vase. Use Delta brand glass paints, available at craft stores or online. Follow the directions on the package to make any design you like. Each color of paint is about $3. You must use the surface conditioner.

☺ ☻ EXPLORATION: The Lion of St. Mark

The Lion of St. Mark is the symbol of Venice. Sometime in the 9th century a couple of Venetian merchants went to Egypt and retrieved the bones of the apostle Mark, who had been buried there. In order to get out of Egypt with their booty, William Lithgow wrote in 1614 . . .

They placed the corpse in a large basket covered with herbs and swine's flesh which the Musselmans [Muslims] hold in horror, and the bearers were directed to cry Khwazir (pork), to all who should ask questions or approach to search. In this manner they reached the vessel. The body was enveloped in the sails, and suspended to the mainmast till the moment of departure, for it was necessary to conceal this precious booty from those who might come to clear the vessel in the roads. At last the Venetians quitted the shore full of joy. They were hardly in the open sea when a great storm arose. We are assured that S. Mark then appeared to the captain and warned him to strike all his sails immediately, lest the ship, driven before the wind, should be wrecked upon hidden rocks. They owned their safety to this miracle.

Ever since, the winged lion of St. Mark has been the symbol of Venice.

Make your own winged lion craft.
1. Paint your hand with yellow paint and press onto a piece of white construction paper to make a handprint.
2. Cut out a circle of yellow construction paper, about 1 ½ inches in diameter. Cut slits all around the edges to make a fringed mane.
3. Draw a face on the construction paper circle and glue it to the handprint, on the end opposite the thumb mark. The fingers become the legs and the thumb is the tail. Now add paper wings to the back of your lion.

☺ ☺ ☻ **EXPLORATION: Alhambra**
Alhambra was a palace and fortress built by the Moors of

Additional Layer

Read about how Jews were treated in Venice during the Middle Ages. http://www.jewishvirtuallibrary.org/jsource/vjw/Venice.html

Jews have been treated horribly through all of history, you could even argue that no other group has ever been as relentlessly oppressed as the Jews. But why? What do you think?

Explanation

Harrison is in his colorful house period. His art may not seem gallery quality to you, but it's teaching early handwriting skills to this little man of mine.

Harrison at four has control and ability over his crayon or pencil at the same level my non-drawers did at years older. His motor control has developed much more quickly due to practice.

So encourage art with your little ones.

Michelle

Additional Layer

Tessellations (complex geometric patterns) found in Alhambra inspired the work of modern artist M.C. Escher.

Famous Folks

El Cid, meaning the lord, is a Spanish folk hero. He fought in the Reconquista against the Moors most successfully.

He also fought the Christian kingdoms on the side of the Moors, it all depended on who was paying more. His sword was named Tizona.

Famous Folks

Bartolomé Bermejo was a Spanish painter of the 15th century. He painted in the Flemish style with lively subjects and glowing oil paints. He was unsurpassed in Spain at this period.

Granada in the 14th and 15th centuries. Its architecture and design are breathtakingly beautiful. Find images of the palace online. Wikipedia has an excellent article for older kids to read.

Make a model building from Alhambra Palace. You need a shoe box and the template from the end of this unit.

1. Cut out and color the template. The building is light tan and the roof is dark brown.
2. Glue it onto the inside bottom of the shoebox. Cut out the inside of the arches.
3. On the remaining surfaces of the inside of the box, paint a large rectangular pool of water in front of the arches and hedges and palm trees on the sides. Around the pool paint light tan colored pavement. Fill in the sky with blue. If you like you can also decorate the outside of the box.

Photo by Jim Gordon and shared under CC license via Wikimedia.

☺ ☻ ☻ EXPLORATION: Reconquista

Make a book showing the reconquest of Spain. Print out the reconquest of Spain maps from the end of this unit, cut it into four pieces along the solid lines and add a cover. Title the book *Reconquista* or *The Reconquest of Spain*. Color the maps on each page.

Older kids can also write a sentence or two describing the map on the blank facing page. They will have to do some research, probably online since there aren't too many books on this subject in most libraries. Include things like which kings and countries led the attacks, which battles were most important, and significant dates.

GEOGRAPHY: SWITZERLAND

Switzerland is a landlocked country in the Alps and nearby plateaus of central Europe. It is a federal republic made up of twenty-six independent cantons. Switzerland is made up of three distinct regions including Germanic, French, and Italian languages and cultures. They share a desire for representative government and a history of aloofness from the affairs of other nations in Europe. Switzerland has not been involved in any war since 1812. They are not a member of the European Union and only became part of the United Nations in 2002.

Photo by Roland Zumbühl and shared under CC licence on Wikimedia.

In spite of being a nation of peace, the Swiss are prepared for war with state of the art technology, equipment and training. Only 5% of the military are full time professionals. The rest of the military is made up of conscripts. Every young man in Switzerland must serve in the military. After a period of training they go on a reserve system, with periodic supplemental training.

Switzerland is a strongly capitalist country with a strong currency and low rates of inflation. They have low tax rates, low regulation, miniscule unemployment, and high wages. Their standard of living is one of the highest in the world. The major industries include tourism, chemicals, real estate, financial services, musical instruments, measuring instruments, and international organization headquarters. They also participate in free trade agreements all over the world. The one place the

Additional Layer

Why do criminal masterminds always have their money in Swiss bank accounts?

The Swiss banks have hundreds of years old policies, codified into law, regarding secrecy of bank accounts. So if I put money in a Swiss bank, it remains secret, no one knows how much or the amount of my transfers, or anything else.

Also, the Swiss are financial geniuses with a stable currency even as surrounding nations grow more and more insolvent. If you put your money in Swiss Franks, it'll still be worth the same amount in ten years.

Further, the Swiss actually have more assets than liabilities, meaning your money will be there, no FDIC insurance necessary.

Finally, the Swiss haven't been involved directly in a war in over 200 years, making the country, as a whole, stable and safe.

Find out what else makes Swiss accounts desirable.

Fabulous Fact
This is the Matterhorn, a famous mountain in the Swiss Alps.

Photo from Zermatt photos and shared under CC license on Wikimedia.

Fabulous Fact

About 80% of the world's watches are made in Switzerland. The Swiss pretty much invented the art of precise measurement and intricate workmanship.

Fabulous Fact
Back in the Middle Ages and up through early modern times if you wanted to travel to Italy, the center of cultural and religious life, you had to walk on foot through the passes in the Swiss Alps.

The Swiss built hostels for travelers to stay in and maintained trails for them to walk on during their journey, but the trail was difficult, even harrowing at times.

market is not free is in health care, which is universally provided by government and, while the Swiss are largely satisfied with the system, it is extremely expensive and rising in cost.

And the most important contribution by the Swiss to the world . . . chocolate of course.

☺ ☺ ☺ **EXPLORATION: Switzerland Map**
Use the map from the end of this unit. The map shows each of the cantons, labeled, and a few of the major cities and lakes. Switzerland is divided into three main languages and cultures – German, French, and Italian. There is a fourth culture, uniquely Swiss in the high mountains toward the south of the country; there the people speak Romansh. Switzerland does not have one united culture like most nations. Color in the four major linguistic and cultural areas of Switzerland as shown below.

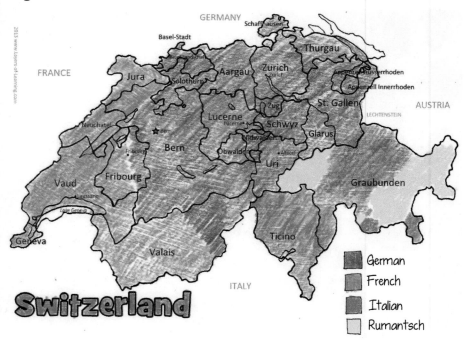

You could also use your student atlas to create an elevation map, showing the mountains, some of the famous peaks, and the passes. Include the major cities to see where they are located, mountains or lowlands.

Map shared under CC license © 2005 swisstopo

☻ **EXPLORATION: Just How Big (or Little) Are You?**
Switzerland measures about 220 miles from east to west, and 140 miles from north to south. That makes it about 1/10 the size of California or the size of New Hampshire and Vermont if you put them together. About 70 percent of that is mountainous. That doesn't leave its 7.3 million people much room for homes! Thousands of their towns snugly fill a narrow plateau between the Alps and the Joura Mountains.

Figure out about how big Switzerland is compared with the state you live in. Sketch your state, then sketch a representation of the size of Switzerland on top of your state.

☻ ☻ ☻ **EXPLORATION: Make Zopf**
Zopf is a special bread eaten for Sunday breakfast.

    2 cups flour
    1 Tbsp. salt
    1 Tbsp. yeast
    1 tsp. sugar
    ½ cup butter, softened
    1 ½ cups milk

Additional Layer

Switzerland's climate is mostly continental temperate, warm summers and cold, snowy winters. At higher elevations it is cold year round with glaciers covering the upper mountain valleys. At the most southern tip of Switzerland the climate is a much warmer Mediterranean heat.

Find out more about what the landscape of Switzerland is like.

Photo by Glaurung and shared under CC license on Wikimedia

Here are Moiry Lake and the Moiry glacier.

Additional Layer

People have a lot of different ideas about what people should eat to stay healthy. There's really only one thing everyone agrees on: what you eat is the most important factor to your overall health; it does matter. Spend some time reading lots of different peoples' ideas on healthy eating and decide for yourself.

The last remaining trace of this is the Swiss Guard that still stands in Vatican City guarding the Pope.

Warm milk on the stove top or in the microwave, until hot, but not boiling. Add yeast and sugar and allow to sit for ten minutes. Add salt, butter, and stir in flour. Knead dough, adding more flour if necessary to make a stiff dough. Let sit for thirty minutes. Knead dough again, adding more flour if necessary. Dough should be moist, but not stick to your hands when working with it. Separate the dough into two parts. Separate each part into three. Roll each of the three sections into a long snake and braid together to form the loaf. Repeat with the second loaf. Place on a greased baking sheet. Allow to rise for 30 more minutes. Brush on egg yolk to the surface of the bread. Bake at 400° F for 45 minutes.

☺ ☺ ☺ EXPLORATION: Make Müesli

Müesli is a Swiss oatmeal. This recipe was introduced by a Swiss doctor, Maxmilian Bircher-Benner, who thought the Swiss ate too much meat, and a diet heavier in fruits, vegetables, and grains was more healthful. This recipe is for one dish. Each person can make their own bowl with exactly the ingredients they like.

1 Tbsp. quick oats
3 Tbsp. water
1 Tbsp. milk or cream
Honey or sugar to taste
(go easy on this one)
1 tsp. lemon juice
Diced or grated apple
(1 whole apple for each person)

Optional ingredients:
   raisins
   berries
   almonds, or other nuts
   bananas
   yogurt
   orange juice

Let the mixture sit about ten minutes to soften and then eat. Serve with hot chocolate.

☺ ☺ EXPLORATION: Switzerland's History

Switzerland's history is fascinating and inspiring. Read *The Apple and The Arrow* by Mary and Conrad Buff. It is the story passed down for generations by the people of Switzerland telling of their resistance to tyranny and their beginnings as an independent nation.

After you've read the story, play a target shooting game. Use small balls or beanbags and aim at a cardboard apple-shaped target.

After you play the game discuss these things about the book:

- Why did William Tell and the other men meet on the mountain top that night?
- What were conditions like for the people of the Swiss Cantons?
- Do you think the Swiss were right to rebel against their government? Why?
- What do you think the bear and the eagle in cages in the village represent?
- Who in the book showed courage and how?
- How did Gessler try to keep control of the people?
- William Tell kills Gessler in the story. Is what he did right or wrong? Why?
- How did the actions of William Tell, a simple woodsman inspire his country?

☺ ☻ EXPLORATION: Flag

The Swiss flag is easy to make. Start with a sheet of paper and use masking tape to cover the cross in the middle. Paint over the whole page with red tempera paint. Once it's dry, remove the tape.

Fabulous Fact
Women were not allowed to vote in Switzerland until 1971, some of the cantons holding out until 1990, but the first woman president was elected in 1999.

Additional Layer
Yodeling isn't unique to the Alps, but it is endemic. Some people believe that yodeling was first used by shepherds in the high mountain valleys to call to their animals or to other shepherds or people in the town. The sound carries far in the thin alpine air and echoes off the mountains in a lovely way. Listen to some yodeling here:

http://youtu.be/67rc96joOz8

And listen to this 11 year old girl, Taylor Ware, yodel in the American western style.

http://youtu.be/zbIHx4YGwR4

Additional Layer
The Swiss require every adult male to serve in the militia. They keep their equipment, including their guns and ammo, at their homes. So nearly every Swiss home has a gun and someone trained to use it. But Switzerland also has almost no gun crime.

Additional Layer
This is the Building in Bern where the Swiss Assembly meets.

Find out more about how the Swiss government is set up. Compare it to the government in your country.

Fabulous Fact
Education in Switzerland is controlled by the individual cantons, not by the federal government. There are public and private schools and a university system.

Homeschooling is frowned on in Switzerland, though allowed in most cantons. Zurich bans homeschooling outright because they claim children are not properly socialized at home.

On the Web
Find out more about cultural traditions of Switzerland.
http://www.myswitzerland.com/en/about-switzerland/culture.html

It is thought that the symbol of the Red Cross (the opposite of the Swiss flag – red cross on white background) was based on the Swiss flag because Switzerland was host to the first Geneva Convention, which established standards for humane treatment of every person during wartime.

☺ ☻ ☻ EXPLORATION: Alpine Horns
Alpine legend has it that these strange instruments have been around since the Middle Ages, and maybe even longer. They were originally used to signal from village to village.
Visit YouTube to hear how these fantastically long instruments sound. This is a good video: http://youtu.be/sM1rG6DJnkw. After you've seen the real thing, go check out how this guy made his own from pvc pipe, duct tape, and a traffic cone: http://youtu.be/G-bvCTVaCko

☺ ☻ ☻ EXPEDITION: The Swiss Guard
This is another virtual expedition, though if given the opportunity, I'd jump at the chance to take a real expedition to Europe! You can go visit the Swiss Guard in Vatican City. There are links about its history, a page featuring the guards' duties and everyday life, and a neat photo gallery: http://www.vatican.va/roman_curia/swiss_guard/

☺ ☻ EXPLORATION: The Glacier Express
The Glacier Express is known as the slowest express train in the world. It connects resorts through the Swiss Alps and, because of the difficult elevation changes, the line uses a rack and pinion system to help the train ascend the upward slopes and also slow the train to a safe speed on the downward slopes. The trip takes 7

½ hours one way, partly because the train travels pretty slowly. The line crosses 291 bridges and goes through 91 tunnels. The rail line also travels through Oberalp Pass year round, which isn't open to cars in the winter time because of the high elevation and treacherous roads.

The Glacier Express, photo shared under CC license by Champer

Use the printable worksheet at the end of this unit to make your own Glacier Express.

☺ ☻ ☻ EXPLORATION: Cable Cars

The Swiss Alps divide a good portion of Europe in two, which makes transportation tricky. Besides trains, cable cars also traverse the high elevations, connecting many stations through the mountains.

Make your own cable car. You'll need a clean, empty half-gallon milk carton, sturdy string, scissors, a craft knife, and paints.

Start by cutting out windows and a door on your milk carton. Also cut small holes in each of the four top corners. Give your cable car a cool paint job. Once it's dry, put a 2 foot length of string through the rear holes, then a second 2 foot length through the front holes.

Now set up your Swiss Alps by setting up two chairs and tying a loop of string around the top. Tie your cable car on. Cable cars aren't independently powered. They are attached to a moving cable, which allows the car to be pulled along.
If you want, you can create mountains around your cable car by

Fabulous Fact

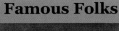

Accordions are also very popular in some parts of Switzerland.

Famous Folks

Paracelcus, named so by himself (his real name was Theophrastus Bombastus von Hohenheim), was a Swiss doctor and alchemist. He lived from 1493 to 1541. His greatest contribution was combining chemistry with medicine.

Additional Layer

Look for Switzerland in the news. What is happening there and what do you think of it?

Famous Folks

Jean-Jacques Rousseau was a Geneva born, French speaking philosopher whose ideas greatly influenced both the American and French revolutions, which in turn influenced most of the rest of the world.

Additional Layer

There are versions of Duck, Duck, Goose played by children all over the world. In Israel it's called "Black Rabbit." In place of saying duck, the kids say "_____ rabbit" (fill in various colors in the blank). Then when they say "Black Rabbit" you must run, just like when we say "goose."

In India it's similar to the Swiss version, except it's a handkerchief that's dropped instead of a rock.

placing blankets around the chairs. You can even craft some little houses, or use toy houses. Then you can transport little toy people in your cable car by pulling on the cable loop.

☺ ☻ EXPLORATION: Don't Look Back, The Fox Walks Around

Kids around the world love playing games, and Swiss kids are no different. Try this Swiss game, reminiscent of our own *Duck, Duck, Goose*. All the kids sit in a circle facing inward, except one child who is the fox. The kids in the circle must not look behind them. The fox holds a small stone and walks around the outside of the circle. The fox discreetly drops the stone behind one child. When the child realizes the stone is behind her, she jumps up and chases the fox around the circle. If she catches him, he must be the fox again. If the fox makes it back to her spot without being caught, she becomes the fox. If the fox makes it all the way around the circle without the child noticing the stone has been dropped, she must sit in the middle of the circle and be the "lazy egg" until another child takes her place as the lazy egg.

☻ EXPLORATION: Castles of Switzerland

Switzerland has some truly gorgeous architecture, including this romantic castle on the shores of Lake Geneva, Château de Chillon. Visit this site: (http://www.myswitzerland.com/en-us/castles-palaces.html) Then choose a castle to do a report on.

SCIENCE: NERVOUS SYSTEM

All those body systems we've learned about in the earlier units need a central command to tell them what to do and how to act. Your brain, spinal cord, and all the nerves in your body are your nervous system. Your nervous system can act automatically for some things and you can also consciously control it for others.

Neurons are special cells that are used in the nervous system. Your brain and your spinal cord are made of trillions of neurons all packed together, and your peripheral nerves are made of long chains of neurons. Each neuron meets at a tiny gap called a, synapse which the electric signal must jump across to reach the next nerve. Neurons can be specialized for certain jobs.

The human brain is one of the most mysterious of our internal organs. Scientists do know that certain parts of the brain

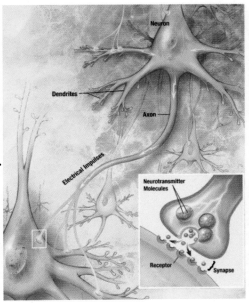

Additional Layer

Drugs, alcohol, physical trauma, poor diet, and lack of use can all damage our brains and make us forgetful, crazy, or less intelligent over time. Discuss the dangers of abusing our bodies through drugs and risky behavior.

Additional Layer

People have oft tried to define what intelligence is. The truth is, there are so many kinds of intelligence to consider, that it's hard to say. Consider these kinds:

Linguistic intelligence
("word smart")
Logical-mathematical intelligence
("number/reasoning smart")
Spatial intelligence
("picture smart")
Bodily-Kinesthetic intelligence
("body smart")
Musical intelligence
("music smart")
Interpersonal intelligence
("people smart")
Intrapersonal intelligence
("self smart")
Naturalist intelligence
("nature smart")

With so many fields of knowledge it's hard to define "smart." I work in education and my husband is a jet pilot. He shouldn't be teaching any more than I should be flying your plane.

function in certain ways and they have made brain maps to show these regions. They also know that people and animals are born with a certain number of brain cells and as we age we lose brain cells, but never make more.

☺ ☻ EXPLORATION: If I Only Had A Brain

Add a brain to your body model you've been working on. It is a very important part, you wouldn't want to leave it off.

☺ ☻ EXPLORATION: Telegraph Line

Look up the Schoolhouse Rock song, *Telegraph Line*. You can find it on video or DVD from your library or on You Tube. It's fun and gives a great basic overview of how the nervous system works. http://youtu.be/3XEoz_rf4oA

☺ ☻ EXPLORATION: Thinking Cap

Get a white swimming cap and outline the brain regions with a black marker. Color in the regions with colored markers and label them. Or leave them unlabeled so you can quiz over them.

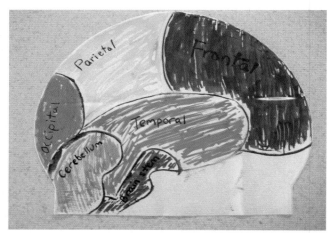

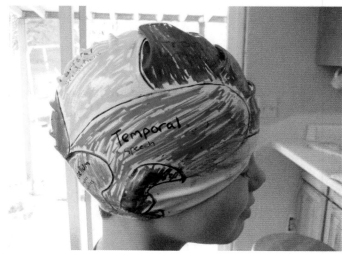

☺ ☻ ☻ EXPLORATION: My Very Own Neuron

Make a model of a neuron. Use salt dough or bake-able clay. After the clay has hardened or cooled (follow directions on bake-able clay package, and allow the salt dough to dry at room temperature for 48 hours) you can paint it and label it. A neuron is one nerve cell. The one showed below is an association neuron in the spinal cord, which passes messages along a long line between the brain and the body parts.

Sculpting a neuron

Here is a very detailed picture of a neuron to use as a reference:

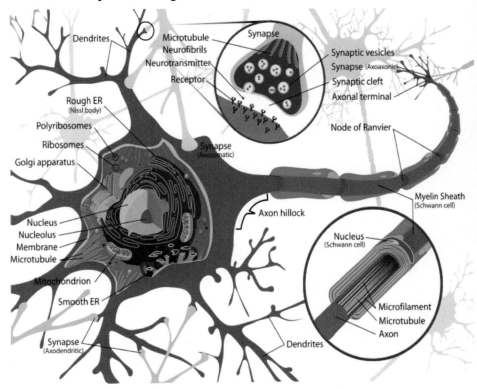

On the Web

Visit Web MD to see pictures of the brain and to explore various brain injuries and conditions. http://www.webmd.com /brain/picture-of-the-brain

Fabulous Facts

A human brain weighs about 3 pounds (that's half the weight of your skin)

Your brain is made up of 75% water.

The brain can't feel pain. It has no pain receptors.

There are 100,000 or so miles of blood vessels in the brain.

Made up of about 60% fat, the brain is the fattiest organ in the human body.

Your brain uses about 25% of the calories your body takes in every day. So think harder and lose weight? That would be nice.

Every time you learn something new, physical or mental, you create new connections in your brain.

On the Web

Here are a whole bunch of brain and nerve coloring sheets for kids. http://faculty.washington.edu/chudler/colorbook.html

On the Web

This You Tube video shows an actual dissection of a human brain from a cadaver. Yeah, so for high school; it's a little much for younger kids.

http://youtu.be/CXGMDdJo6HQ

Additional Layer

Our brains are super complex, super durable, and incredible at learning. But the brain has a few quirks too. NASA performed an experiment in space. It was simple. Astronauts just had to catch a ball that was thrown at them. They could do it, but their timing was a little off. They were expecting gravity when there was none. The body adapts within a few days to other aspects of weightlessness but the expectation of gravity persisted for more than two weeks. Read more about the experiment: http://science.nasa.gov/science-news/science-at-nasa/2002/18mar_playingcatch/

It's a Funny!

Check out these corny neuroscience jokes!

http://faculty.washington.edu/chudler/jokes.html

☺ ☻ ☻ **EXPLORATION: Label The Neuron**

Use the worksheet from the end of this unit and label the neuron by cutting and pasting the appropriate labels on to the diagram.

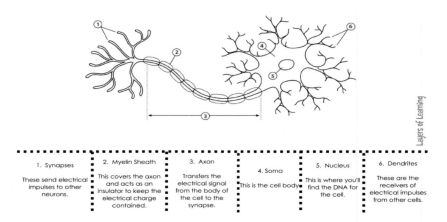

Label The Neuron

Cut apart the labels from the bottom of the worksheet. Glue each one down to the diagram in its appropriate place.

1. Synapses	2. Myelin Sheath	3. Axon	4. Soma	5. Nucleus	6. Dendrites
These send electrical impulses to other neurons.	This covers the axon and acts as an insulator to keep the electrical charge contained.	Transfers the electrical signal from the body of the cell to the synapse.	This is the cell body	This is where you'll find the DNA for the cell.	These are the receivers of electrical impulses from other cells.

☺ ☻ ☻ **EXPLORATION: Making Connections**

Draw ten dots down each side of a piece of paper or on a white board. From each dot on the left, draw one line to each dot on the right. Use a different color for each dot on the left. This represents each neuron making ten connections. It gets pretty complicated with lines criss-crossing every where.

The reality is even more surprising though. Each neuron probably makes thousands of connections with other neurons. Connections are formed when your brain must perform tasks. The more you learn and exercise your brain and your body, the more connections you will make.

☺ ☻ **EXPERIMENT: Protected Brain**

Your brain is extremely important, so it is protected by a skull and also by a fluid called Cerebrospinal Fluid, a watery stuff that is all around your brain inside your skull.

1. To see how it works, get an egg. The egg is your brain. Drop it on a counter top from a few inches height. Broken egg.
2. Now get a plastic container, just larger than an egg and put a second egg in. The plastic container represents the skull. Drop it to the counter from the same height. Observe the damage to the egg.
3. Get a third egg and place it in the container which is also filled with water. The water represents the cerebrospinal

fluid. Seal the lid securely. Drop it again from the same height. What damage this time?

Which way was the egg brain protected best?

☺ ☻ EXPLORATION: Brainy Games
Play games to challenge your brain.

- Write a series of color words in colored markers that do not match the word like: RED, BLUE, PURPLE, BLACK, GREEN, ORANGE, and so on. Try to say the colors (not the words) fast. How does your brain mess up the message?
- How good is your memory? Get a tray of at least ten small objects. Show them for 30 seconds, then cover them up. How many can you remember?
- Here's another variation on the memory game. Have someone walk casually through the room. After they leave see how many details the kids can remember. How tall? What color hair? What color shirt? Were they wearing any jewelry? What color eyes did the person have? Did they have any scars or anything else that identified them?
- How fast can you react? Play red light green light and see who can react the quickest. Have all the players start at one end of a yard or room. The leader yells "green light" and all the players move toward the opposite end. When the leader yells "red light" players must stop.

☺ ☻ EXPERIMENT: Brain Surgery
Dissect a sheep brain. Purchase a dissection kit and guide from a science supplier like Carolina Biological Supply or Home Science Tools.

☺ ☻ EXPERIMENT: Virtual Split Brain Experiment
This one is cool. It shows the procedure that scientists actually went through when they performed the Nobel Prize Winning experiments on people who had their brains split because of epilepsy. The results are weird and they give clues as to how our brains are wired. You get to perform the experiment – virtually.

http://www.nobelprize.org/educational/medicine/split-brain/about.html

☺ EXPLORATION: Color A Brain
Younger kids may enjoy the brain coloring sheet you'll find at the end of this unit.

Additional Layer
A doctor once accidentally punctured the sack that holds the cerebrospinal fluid in my brain and spinal column during a routine procedure. With the sack leaking, the fluid drained out, leaving my brain unsupported. I experienced terrible headaches for days any time I was upright. They eventually patched the leak, my body replenished the cerebrospinal fluid on its own, and I recovered quickly.

Find out some other ailments that can affect your brain.

Additional Layer

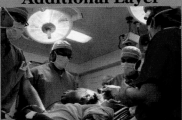

Find out what it takes to become a brain surgeon. How many years of college and training are required? What universities and programs offer this training? How much does it cost? What is the average salary of a brain surgeon? Would you want to be responsible for the welfare of someone else's brain during surgery?

THE ARTS: VAN EYCK & OIL PAINTS

Jan van Eyck was one of the few painters of his time who was wealthy because of his painting. Most painters, even the ones we consider to be truly great, were not nearly as well known during their lives, and they certainly weren't wealthy from their work. Van Eyck was different. He worked for Philip the Good, the Duke of Burgundy, and was handsomely paid for his art. Philip was known for his extravagance and style, and had many composers and artists in his employ. Van Eyck was learned, familiar with classic art and literature, and studied painting. He was considered to be one of the prime painters of his day, maybe even the best. He was also different in another way – at the time the most famous and best painters were from Italy, but Jan van Eyck was from the Netherlands.

This is probably a self portrait of van Eyck.

A myth began long, long ago that he was the inventor of oil paints. Truthfully, oil paints themselves had been around for centuries, but they weren't terribly popular. Up until van Eyck, they were used mostly to paint shields, pottery, and other items, but not for painting art panels. Jan van Eyck began using them to paint his works on wood panels. He became a master of oil painting techniques, and made them look more beautiful and striking than the tempera paints other artists were using. It wasn't long before oil paints on canvas were the standard medium of all the great Renaissance painters.

☺ ☻ ☻ EXPLORATION: Painting Detective

When we look at a painting, we get to act like a detective. First, we learn the basic facts. Who painted it? When? Where? Were they hired by someone to do it? Next, we likely try to discover

Famous Folks

Robert Campin, also known as the Master of Flémalle preceded Jan van Eyck as the greatest Flemish master painter. He also was a favorite of the Burgundians.

Here are some of his:

Portrait of a Woman

Annunciation

Additional Layer

The inscription painted above the mirror says "Jan van Eyck was here 1434." (written in Latin). What a terrific way to sign a painting.

Additional Layer

The court of Burgundy encouraged music as much as art. Adrien Basin was one of the court singers. He composed many songs and was hugely popular, some of his pieces were distributed all over Europe in a time when this was rare due to lack of printing. Basin was part of the Burgundian School of Music. This musical movement gave rise to the Renaissance music styles.

On The Web

Here is some music by Guillaume Dufay, one of the most famous of the Burgundian School: http://youtu.be/gEOGZo o5CvQ

This is a Van Eyck portrait of a man thought to be Guillaume Dufay.

what it's about. Sometimes the story is clear, but quite often, there are hidden meanings. Next, we can analyze techniques the painter used. We look at line, shape, color, balance, unity, and other elements. Finally, we get to say what we think. This has nothing to do with historians, experts, or anyone but ourselves. Every patron of the arts is entitled to his own opinion, and this part of the analysis is the time to share it.

Let's take a look at The Arnolfini Portrait, one of Jan van Eyck's most famous paintings.

1. The basic facts
    Well, we know it was painted by Jan van Eyck. This was a portrait he did of a prominent and wealthy banker from Italy named Arnolfini. It is sometimes thought to be a wedding portrait, though that has been disputed. It was painted in 1434 and was done in oil paints on an oak panel of wood.
2. What is it about?
    Sometimes the story of a painting is clear, but we also have to do a lot of guessing. This clearly seems to be a couple. They are standing in their home and are surrounded by lavish possessions. Their clothing is made of fine silk. He wears a fur cape. The chandelier, fancy carpet, glass windows, and beautiful mirror would only be found in an expensive home at the time. If you look closely you'll also see oranges sitting on the table behind Arnolfini – these were a rare fruit; not just anyone would have them in their possession.

After we see the main subjects, we can dig even deeper to look at the symbolism in a painting. This painting is full of symbols that probably represent deeper meanings. Let's take a look at some:

*   The dog probably represents loyalty and fidelity between the couple.
*   The string of beads on the wall is actually a set of rosary beads, used to count prayers. This would have represented their devotion to God.
*   Look closely at the chandelier. How many candles are lit? Just one. One lit candle represented the presence of God.
*   The mirror is particularly interesting. Besides the fact that mirrors were rare, this one is also adorned with scenes from the life of Christ. Each of the round decorations is actually a miniature scene. If you look into the mirror you see not only the backs of Arnolfini

and his wife, but also two more people standing there. Most scholars believe one of these people represents van Eyck. Some (the same ones who think this is a wedding portrait) think this represents the two witnesses of the wedding. Regardless of if this was a wedding or not, the couple were clearly religious as there are a lot of religious symbols present.

- The portrait also shows various signs of fertility. The woman looks pregnant, but most likely she was not. Fertility was prized, so often women were portrayed that way. A high waist with bustling skirt was also the style of the time, so this would have been fashionable. The red bed linens were also a sign of fertility as red beds were associated with birthing chambers. The carving on the chair is also of St. Margaret, the patron saint of childbirth.

3. Techniques of the painter
   Jan van Eyck truly was a master. The portrait is beautifully balanced and full of movement. Your eye is led all around the painting, beginning with the couple and the grasp of their hands. Next, your eye is led to the center – the mirror, and then up to the chandelier. Finally, you'll see the many details in the background that tell the rest of the story about the couple.

   One of the most astounding achievements of Van Eyck was his use of light. Look at the light as it shines in through the window. Can you see some things it is reflecting on? You can see the glimmers of light on the chandelier, the mirror, the faces of the man and woman, and even on the tiny, detailed hairs of the dog. The highlights and shadows look almost like a photograph. He achieved this by painting many layers of oil paints.

4. What do YOU think?
   I could tell you what I think, but that doesn't really matter. What matters is what you think. Do you like it? Why? What does it make you think of? What do you think the people are thinking?

☺ ☺ ☺ EXPEDITION: Virtual Van Eyck
Go on a virtual tour of some of Jan van Eyck's paintings. Visit www.museumsyndicate.com, click on painters, then scroll down to van Eyck, Jan. You can tour many of his paintings. Try analyzing several more and share your opinions.

☺ ☺ ☺ EXPLORATION: Oil Paints
One of the main differences between tempera paints and oil

Famous Folks
Rogier van der Weyden was court painter for a time to Philip the Good of Burgundy and took over Jan van Eyck's earlier popularity. He was nearly forgotten by the 17th century, and only lately rediscovered.

This painting of the Virgin and Child is by him.

On the Web
Try this online jigsaw puzzle of the Arnolfini Marriage. Search for "Arnolfini Marriage Jigsaw Puzzle."

Tip
Many painters set up their palette just like the color wheel. They also color mix according to the color wheel.

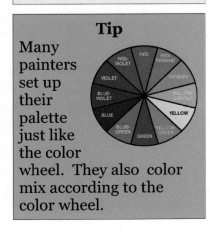

Fabulous Fact

Vincent Van Gogh, Claude Monet, Leonardo daVinci, Pablo Picasso – most of the big name painters you've heard of were all master oil painters. Some of them used other media as well though. DaVinci is almost as famous for his sketches as he is for the Mona Lisa.

Additional Layer

At first oil paints were done on wood panels. It wasn't long before canvas became the new favorite though. Canvas was smoother and easier to work with, but mostly, it was a lot lighter to carry around.

paints is the drying time. It takes oil paints much longer to dry, so artists began to utilize that extra time to play with the paints on the canvas and manipulate them into intricate details. Try squirting several colors of oil paints on a wood panel or canvas. Use various brushes and tools to play with the paints. Make them swirl. Try creating zigzags or other lines. Use a brush with only one or two bristles to create tiny lines, like hairs. What happens when you layer colors on top of each other? Try putting a light color thinly on top of a more bold color. Experiment and have fun.

☺ ☻ ☻ EXPLORATION: Light

Oil paints have one other really important difference from tempera paints. They are translucent, meaning that light can pass through them. This was how painters began to show light reflecting within paintings in the Renaissance. They painted the solid colors, then added extra layers of lighter paint over the top for the lit areas and extra layers of blue tones over the top for the shadowy areas, allowing the colors underneath to still show through.

Paint an outdoor scene. Once it is completely dry, go back over the painting adding light and shadows in. This takes years for artists to master, and some never do, but whether or not it's perfect, it's still a neat exploration of how oil paints can be used in this way.

☺ ☻ ☻ EXPLORATION: Who I Am

Portraits are pictures of people. Self-portraits are pictures of yourself. Paint or draw a self-portrait. You can include your whole body or just show a bust of your face and shoulders. In Jan van Eyck's day often artists included items in the portrait to tell more about who a person was. Include some objects that tell what kind of a person you are and what your interests are. My self-portrait would probably include lots of flowers and plants because I love to garden, a globe because I travel a lot, a piano because I am a piano teacher, and piles of books since most of my free time is spent reading. Include some items in your self-portrait that tell about who you are.

When Van Gogh painted this portrait of himself he included his easel and oil paints. They helped define who he was. What defines you?

☺ ☻ EXPLORATION: Signing the Frame
Painters often used to craft the frame their paintings resided in. They painted on wood panels or canvas, then mounted their work in frames and signed the frames. It was thought of as a whole piece of art once it was framed. Get an inexpensive wood frame (I've seen them at dollar stores and also in the craft section of Wal-Mart for a dollar) and frame a painting you've done. Paint the frame to compliment the picture and sign the frame rather than your painting.

☻ EXPLORATION: Oil Painting Tutorial
You Tube has some excellent painting tutorials for beginners made by artists. Here's one nice simple tutorial that I thought, hey, even I could do that! http://youtu.be/gLk78Kc9EMU

This video is the first in a series. If you get interested in oil painting you can find many more tutorials; it's like having an art teacher at your house.

Here is another good tutorial series for beginners: http://youtu.be/8NVVTeDHNks

Before you start you need a prepared canvas, a set of oil paints, linseed oil (to soften and wet the oil paints), a palette (any smooth board covered with wax paper, taped on), and a variety of brushes. In oil painting in particular it's important to have an

Additional Layer
Which is the most stolen and vandalized piece of art in the entire world? Read here to find out: http://secrethistoryofart. blogspot.com/2010/11/v an-eycks-ghent-altarpiece.html

Additional Layer
At first many painters started using oil paints over their tempera paints as a glaze, but eventually most Renaissance artists were using solely oil paints as they better learned to work with them.

Madonna von Lucca, van Eyck (1430)

Writer's Workshop
Imagine what it would be like to be a painter like Jan van Eyck, working for royals and important people and painting their portraits. Write a day-in-the-life journal entry about what you imagine of his life.

What Makes Oil Paints Special?

Oil paints combine extraordinary realism with brilliant color. The paints are very flexible so they can be applied in both thick, textured brushstrokes and thin, fine detail. They also dry very slowly, allowing artists to mix larger batches of paint and keep them for more than one painting session. Slow drying paint can be carefully blended to make soft, seamless shadows that give the painted objects a three dimensional form. The oil in oil paint makes pigments translucent, allowing artists to apply colors in thin layers or glazes, generating rich, glowing colors.

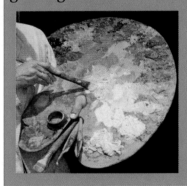

Fabulous Fact

Some painters don't even bother with brushes all the time. They use knives and other cutlery, and yes, even their own fingers to manipulate the paint on the canvas.

easel. But this can just be a board propped up. Finally, you need a solvent to clean your brushes in.

My sister-in-law wanted to learn to oil paint when she was a kid. She painted this ocean scene when she was 10 years old.

☺ ☻ EXPLORATION: Blending

One of the most interesting things about oil paints is the way they blend. For this exploration you'll need a pencil, tempera paints, oil paints, linseed oil, brushes, and water.

Begin by drawing 5 boxes on your paper. Each one should be between an inch and two inches long. Label them according to the diagram below. Now choose two colors of paints to work with from each medium. Start by filling in the tempera paint box with your first color of temperas, then fill in the oil box with the same color of oil paints. Also fill in the oil glaze box with the same oil paints. In the oil blend square, you'll paint half of the box with the same oil paints. Now completely clean the oil paint brush using the linseed oil and apply the second color on the other half. Gently blend the two in the middle with the brush. Do this on the tempera blend box with the tempera paints, using water to clean the brush rather than linseed oil. Once the oil glazing square is dry, thin the second oil color with some of the linseed oil and paint a light glaze over part of the square.

Tempera   **Temp. Blend**   **Oil**   **Oil Blend**   **Oil Glazing**

Discuss the techniques and the way they look. Continue to experiment with both kinds of paints and see what kinds of textures, light, and shadows you can create. Which paint do you prefer to work with?

☻ ☻ EXPLORATION: Cracking

If you've ever seen an old oil painting covered with thin, hairlike cracks, you've probably wondered – is the painting broken? The cracking comes because oil paint shrinks as it dries. Oil paint that is applied thickly may shrink so much that it cracks as it dries. If the first layer of paint is very thick, and thin layers

are painted on top of it before it is totally dry, it will crack all the layers applied thereafter. As the paint continues to dry, the cracks will get bigger.

Try it out. Spread a thick layer of oil paint on smooth wood, let it sit for a bit, but then paint thin layers over the top before the under layer is completely dry. Now watch as it dries. Chances are, it will crack, though it may take some time.

As artists gained more experience working with oil paint, they learned to prevent cracking by painting thin, fast drying layers first and leaving the thick, slow drying layers for last.

Explanation

The idea of learning to oil paint may seem overwhelming if you're new to it, but it's not as daunting as you might think. My mother-in-law watched an oil painter giving instruction on television and was able to create this snowy scene from his tutorial.

Oil paints are actually pretty forgiving since you can always just add another layer of paint to cover up mistakes.

The supplies aren't terribly expensive either. For less that $10 you can get a starter set of paints. You can practice on watercolor paper if you aren't ready for a canvas.

Coming up next . . .

Unit 2-II

Wars of the Roses
Russia – Health
Minstrels & Plays

My Ideas For This Unit:

Title: _____   Topic: _____

_____

_____

_____

_____

_____

_____

_____

_____

Title: _____   Topic: _____

_____

_____

_____

_____

_____

_____

_____

_____

_____

Title: _____   Topic: _____

_____

_____

_____

_____

_____

_____

_____

_____

My Ideas For This Unit:

Title: _____   Topic: _____

_____

_____

_____

_____

_____

_____

_____

_____

Title: _____   Topic: _____

_____

_____

_____

_____

_____

_____

_____

_____

_____

_____

Title: _____   Topic: _____

_____

_____

_____

_____

_____

_____

_____

_____

Venetian Gondola

This is a gondola in Venice. Most of the streets of Venice are actually canals of water. The Gondolas are used as transportation around the city. This gondola is carrying a wealthy woman to her destination, perhaps the house of a friend, the theater, shopping, or to one of the cathedrals of the city. Venice was one of the wealthiest cities in all the world during the late Middle Ages.

Burgundy, Venice, Spain: Unit 2-10

1204 2-10
Venice finances the Fourth Crusade and makes a killing

1248 2-10
Reconquista
722-1492

Christians reconquer most of Spain

1303 2-10
Crossbow proficiency by all adult males in Venice compulsory

1363-1304 2-10
Duke Philippe the Good of Burgundy rules

1348 2-10
Black Death devastates Venice

1381 2-10
Venice defeats Genoa to control all Mediterranean trade

1410-1411 2-10
Burgundy wars with Armagnac

1419 2-10
Duke Jean the Fearless of Burgundy is murdered

1450 2-10
Venice has over 3,000 merchant ships, fitted out for war when necessary

1469 2-10
Isabella and Ferdinand of Spain marry

1474 2-10
Isabella and Ferdinand co-rule Castile

1477 2-10
Marie of Burgundy marries Maximilian of Austria

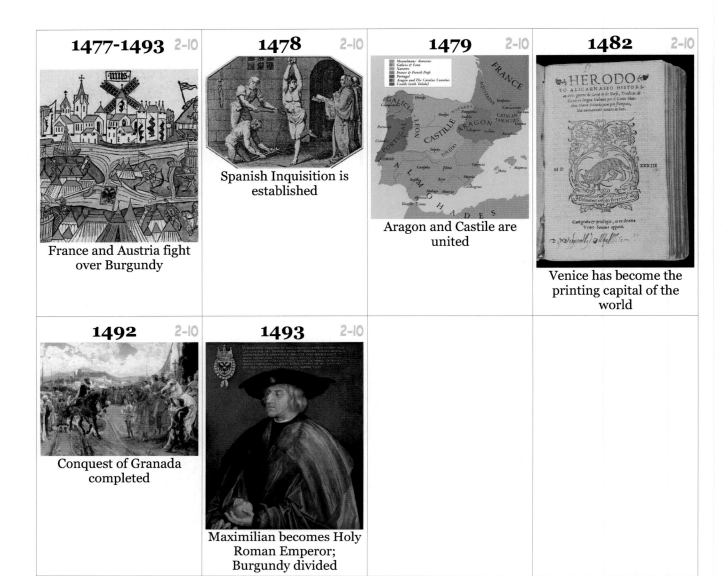

France and Austria fight over Burgundy

Spanish Inquisition is established

Aragon and Castile are united

Venice has become the printing capital of the world

Conquest of Granada completed

Maximilian becomes Holy Roman Emperor; Burgundy divided

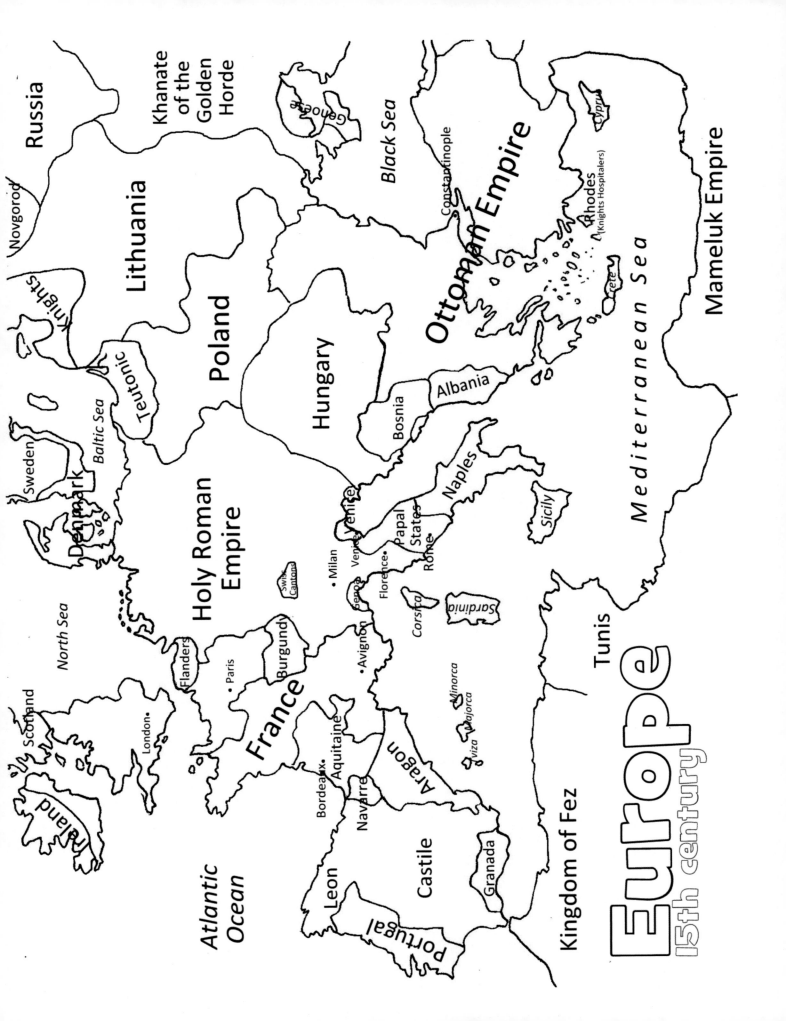

Europe
15th century

Venice

Territories and Trade
15th-16th Century

Venice•

Venetian
Territories

○ Important
Venetian
Trade Port

→ Trade Route

Alhambra

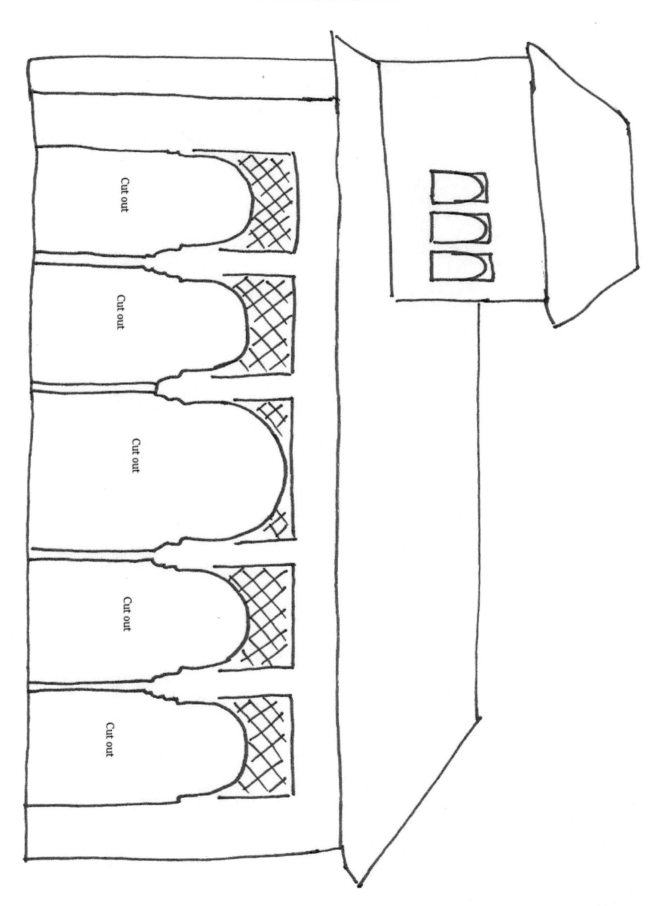

Reconquest of Spain Maps

900 AD

1300 AD

790 AD

1150 AD

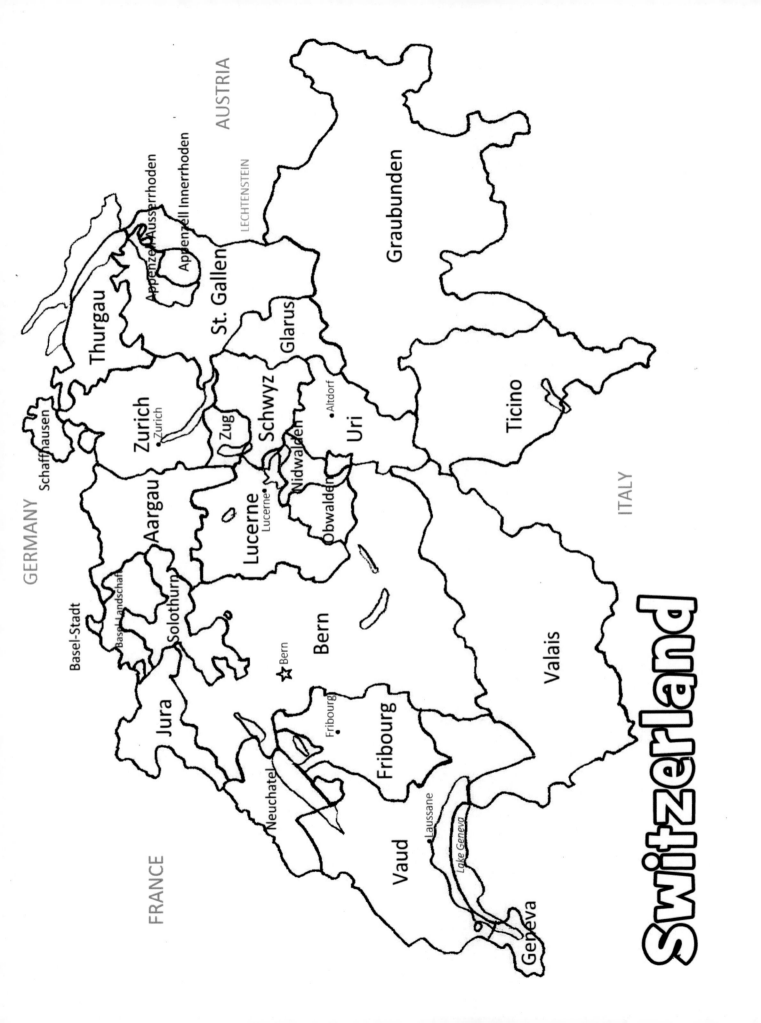

The Glacier Express

The slowest express train in the world

Draw more train cars on the Glacier Express. Now color the cars. Draw and color the Alps mountains of Switzerland in the background of your picture. Include facts you learned about the train around your picture, or write a paragraph about it on the back.

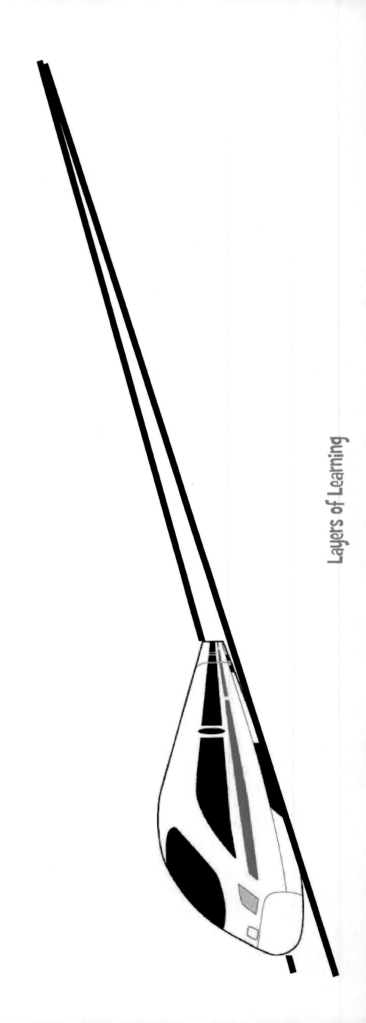

Label The Neuron

Cut apart the labels from the bottom of the worksheet. Glue each one down to the diagram in its appropriate place.

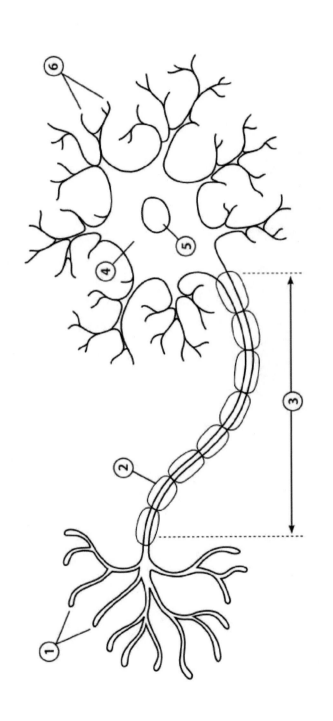

1. Synapses	2. Myelin Sheath	3. Axon	4. Soma	5. Nucleus	6. Dendrites
These send electrical impulses to other neurons.	This covers the axon and acts as an insulator to keep the electrical charge contained.	Transfers the electrical signal from the body of the cell to the synapse.	This is the cell body.	This is where you'll find the DNA for the cell.	These are the receivers of electrical impulses from other cells.

Color The Brain

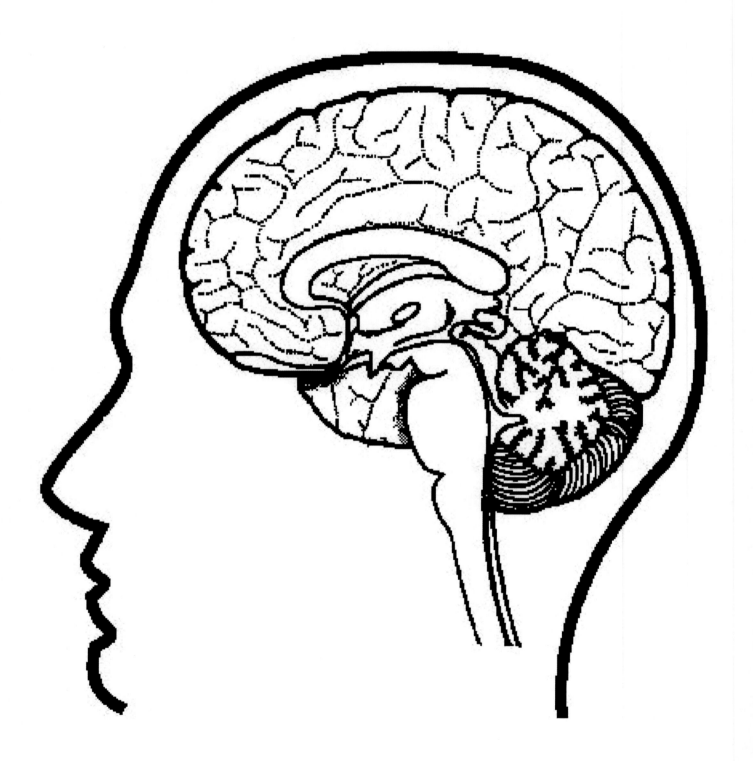

ABOUT THE AUTHORS

Karen & Michelle . . .
Mothers, sisters, teachers, women who are passionate
about educating kids.
We are dedicated to lifelong learning.

Karen, a mother of four, who has homeschooled her kids for more than eight years with her husband, Bob, has a bachelor's degree in child development with an emphasis in education. She lives in Utah where she gardens, teaches piano, and plays an excruciating number of board games with her kids. Karen is our resident Arts expert and English guru {most necessary as Michelle regularly and carelessly mangles the English language and occasionally steps over the bounds of polite society}.

Michelle and her husband, Cameron, homeschooling now for over a decade, teach their six boys on their ten acres in beautiful Idaho country. Michelle earned a bachelor's in biology, making her the resident Science expert, though she is mocked by her friends for being the *Botanist with the Black Thumb of Death*. She also is the go-to for History and Government. She believes in staying up late, hot chocolate, and a no whining policy. We both pitch in on Geography, in case you were wondering, and are on a continual quest for knowledge.

Visit our constantly updated blog for tons of free ideas,
free printables, and more cool stuff for sale:
www.Layers-of-Learning.com

Made in the USA
Middletown, DE
04 April 2025

73769527R00033